Chapter 1: Introduction to AI

🔴 What Is Artificial Intelligence?

Artificial Intelligence (AI) refers to the simulation of human intelligence processes by machines. These include learning, reasoning, problem-solving, perception, and language understanding.

AI is not just robots — it's in the apps you use daily, the recommendations you get, your phone assistant, and even your smart home gadgets.

🔍 Key Components of AI:

- **Learning**: Gaining information and rules to use it.

- **Reasoning**: Using the rules to reach conclusions.

- **Self-correction**: Adjusting based on outcomes.

- **Perception**: Interpreting the world using sensors.

🔦 Real-Life Examples of AI You Already Use

AI Tool	What It Does
Siri / Alexa / Google Assistant	Voice-controlled AI
Google Maps	Predictive routing and traffic
Netflix / YouTube	Recommendation systems
Facebook / Instagram	Face detection and feed curation
Gmail	Smart email categorization

● Why Is AI Important?

- **Saves time**: Automates repetitive tasks

- **Boosts productivity**: Helps with research, writing, and planning

- **Improves decisions**: Based on data, not just instinct

- **Creates opportunities**: From personal finance to business automation

---

● How You'll Use AI Through This Book

This book is a practical guide. After each chapter, you'll:

- Learn about real AI tools

- Understand where they fit in your life or business

- Get actionable ways to use them

- Be able to apply them immediately

■ Chapter 2: Understanding AI Terminology

Understanding AI can feel like learning a new language. In this chapter, we'll break down the **key terms** you'll hear in AI conversations—so you can speak the language confidently, even if you're a complete beginner.

■ The Most Important AI Terms (Made Simple)

Term	Meaning	Real-World Example
AI (Artificial Intelligence)	Software that mimics human thinking	Siri, Alexa, Gmail autocomplete
ML (Machine Learning)	AI that learns from data to improve over time	Spotify learning your music taste
Deep Learning	A form of ML that uses "neural networks" like the brain	Tesla's self-driving tech
NLP (Natural Language Processing)	Allows AI to understand and respond in human language	ChatGPT, Grammarly
Generative AI	AI that can **create** text, images, music, and more	DALL·E, Midjourney, Bard

🔍 Let's Dig a Little Deeper

🔴 Artificial Intelligence (AI)

The broadest term. AI refers to machines doing tasks that normally require human intelligence, like solving problems, recognizing speech, or translating languages.

■ Machine Learning (ML)

A subset of AI. ML algorithms use **data** to make predictions or decisions without being explicitly programmed. The more data you feed them, the better they perform.

🔗 Deep Learning

A more advanced form of ML using layered "neural networks" that simulate how the brain works. Great for image and speech recognition.

💬 Natural Language Processing (NLP)

AI that helps machines understand, interpret, and respond to human language. It powers chatbots, voice assistants, and content tools.

🗯 Generative AI

This AI doesn't just understand—it **creates.** It can generate blog posts, poems, designs, music, and even computer code.

💡 Bonus: Other Popular Terms

Term	Description
Large Language Model (LLM)	AI trained on tons of text data (e.g., ChatGPT is an LLM)
Prompt Engineering	Crafting effective prompts to get the best results from AI
Supervised Learning	ML that learns from labeled data
Unsupervised Learning	ML that finds patterns in data without labels
Reinforcement Learning	AI that learns by trial and error (used in gaming & robotics)

🔧 Real Tools Using These Terms

Concept	Tools
NLP	ChatGPT, Google Translate, Grammarly
Generative AI	Midjourney (images), Soundraw (music), Writesonic (content)
ML & Deep Learning	Tesla Autopilot, Google Lens, YouTube recommendations

■ Chapter 3: Everyday AI Tools for Personal Use

In this chapter, we'll explore **AI tools** that can make your everyday life easier, more efficient, and enjoyable. From managing your schedule to improving your writing, these tools have you covered.

💼 Top AI Tools for Personal Productivity

Tool	What It Does	How You Can Use It
ChatGPT	AI-powered chatbot that generates human-like text	Write emails, brainstorm ideas, get quick summaries
Grammarly	Writing assistant for grammar, spelling, and style	Write better emails, blog posts, social media updates
Notion AI	All-in-one workspace with AI-enhanced note-taking	Organize tasks, manage projects, write blog drafts
Google Assistant	Voice-activated assistant that helps with everyday tasks	Set reminders, send texts, check the weather
Otter.ai	Transcribes meetings and conversations in real-time	Convert voice memos into text, generate summaries

■ AI Tools for Organization

1. Notion AI: Your Digital Organizer

Notion combines note-taking with powerful organization features. The AI inside Notion helps you:

- Summarize long articles

- Generate to-do lists

- Organize thoughts into structured ideas

- Draft blog posts or work reports

How You Can Use It:

- Plan your week's tasks

- Write summaries from research

- Keep track of your goals and projects

2. Google Assistant: Your Voice Assistant

Google Assistant can help you automate daily tasks with voice commands. From setting alarms to managing your calendar, it's like having a personal assistant in your pocket.

How You Can Use It:

- Set reminders to stay on track

- Ask it to send text messages or make calls

- Use it to check weather, news, or sports scores

■ AI for Content Creation and Communication

1. Grammarly: A Better Way to Write

Grammarly is a writing assistant that corrects grammar, spelling, punctuation, and even style. It's like having a professional editor at your fingertips. It also suggests ways to improve the tone, making your writing sound more formal, casual, or conversational as needed.

How You Can Use It:

- Write professional emails or social media posts

- Improve your essays or research papers

- Polish your blog posts before publishing

2. ChatGPT: Writing & Creativity

ChatGPT can help you with everything from writing blog posts to coming up with creative ideas for your projects. It can generate summaries, write articles, answer questions, and even act as a creative writing assistant.

How You Can Use It:

- Generate blog post drafts in seconds

- Brainstorm creative ideas for writing or social media content

- Get detailed answers to complex questions quickly

🪶 AI for Travel and Lifestyle

1. TripIt

TripIt is an AI tool for organizing your travel plans. It automatically generates a travel itinerary by pulling details from your emails and sending you reminders about flights, hotels, and car rentals.

How You Can Use It:

- Plan trips without the hassle of managing multiple bookings

- Sync travel details across your devices

- Get reminders for your flight or hotel check-ins

2. Airbnb and Hotel Recommendation Algorithms

Platforms like Airbnb use AI to personalize recommendations based on your preferences, location, and budget. The AI learns your likes and dislikes, making future travel searches quicker and more accurate.

How You Can Use It:

- Find vacation homes, hotels, or unique stays that match your needs

- Get personalized travel suggestions based on past bookings

⚑ Bonus Tip: Stay Safe with AI

Many AI tools are designed to improve your security:

- **Google Alerts:** Get notified about your name or brand to monitor online mentions.

- **AI-based Security Cameras:** Tools like Nest and Ring use AI to detect faces and potential threats.

■ Summary: Why These Tools Matter

By integrating AI into your personal life, you can:

- Save time on routine tasks

- Stay organized and focused

- Improve the quality of your work and communication

- Access personalized recommendations for travel, lifestyle, and beyond

◼ Chapter 4: AI Tools for Business

AI tools aren't just for personal use; they can transform how businesses operate. In this chapter, we'll explore some of the best AI tools for entrepreneurs, small businesses, and large corporations to automate tasks, boost productivity, and optimize decision-making.

🛠 AI Tools to Boost Productivity in Business

Tool	What It Does	How It Can Help Your Business
Jasper AI	Content creation tool for marketing	Generate blog posts, social media updates, and product descriptions
Copy.ai	AI-powered copywriting assistant	Write compelling ads, landing pages, and sales emails
Surfer SEO	AI for SEO optimization	Improve search engine rankings by optimizing content for SEO
HubSpot CRM	AI-driven customer relationship management	Automate email marketing, manage leads, track customer interactions
Zapier	Automate workflows between apps	Connect tools and automate tasks like data entry, customer onboarding, etc.

💡 AI Tools for Marketing

1. Jasper AI: Content Creation for Marketers

Jasper is an AI tool that helps marketers quickly generate high-quality content, including blog posts, landing pages, and social media posts. It's perfect for businesses looking to scale content production without hiring a full team.

How You Can Use It:

- Write blog posts or email newsletters in minutes

- Generate SEO-optimized content

- Personalize your messages for specific customer segments

2. Copy.ai: Automate Your Marketing Copy

Copy.ai allows you to create effective marketing copy using AI. Whether you need a catchy tagline or a complete product description, this tool helps you write persuasive content quickly.

How You Can Use It:

- Write ad copy, product descriptions, and email templates

- Generate creative and engaging social media posts

- Customize the tone and style to fit your brand's voice

👤 AI for Business Operations and CRM

1. HubSpot CRM: AI-Powered Sales Tools

HubSpot is a leading customer relationship management (CRM) tool, and its AI features allow you to manage contacts, automate follow-ups, track customer interactions, and improve your sales process.

How You Can Use It:

- Use automated workflows to nurture leads and keep customers engaged

- Analyze data to improve customer retention and experience

- Track interactions and set reminders for follow-ups

2. Trello + Butler: Automating Project Management

Trello is a popular project management tool, and Butler (its built-in automation tool) uses AI to automate repetitive tasks. You can set triggers to automatically move cards, assign tasks, and more.

How You Can Use It:

- Automate task assignment based on project stages

- Send notifications when deadlines are approaching

- Integrate with Slack, Google Drive, and more for seamless teamwork

---

🔍 AI for Customer Support

1. Zendesk + AI Chatbots

Zendesk uses AI to help customer service teams provide faster and more efficient support. With AI-driven ticketing systems, automated replies, and chatbots, Zendesk helps businesses streamline customer service.

How You Can Use It:

- Set up automated replies for common customer inquiries

- Use chatbots for 24/7 support and route complex queries to human agents

- Analyze support data to improve service quality and response times

2. Drift: AI for Sales Conversations

Drift is an AI-powered conversational marketing tool. It helps businesses engage with potential customers via live chat or chatbots, qualifying leads, answering queries, and setting up appointments.

How You Can Use It:

- Automate lead qualification and customer interaction

- Set up personalized conversations based on visitor behavior

- Schedule meetings and follow-ups directly in the chat

⬛ AI for Data Analytics

1. Tableau + AI: Data Visualization

Tableau is a powerful data visualization tool, and its AI capabilities make it easier to analyze business data and uncover insights. It can automatically generate reports and suggest ways to visualize your data effectively.

How You Can Use It:

- Visualize your business performance using charts and graphs

- Get AI-driven insights into customer behavior and sales trends

- Create interactive dashboards for team collaboration

2. Google Analytics + AI Insights

Google Analytics uses AI to track website visitors, user behavior, and sales conversions. With AI-powered insights, you can improve your marketing strategy and website performance.

How You Can Use It:

- Track how users engage with your website and products

- Get recommendations on improving site performance

- Monitor campaign performance and adjust strategies in real-time

---

💼 AI Tools for Finance and Accounting

1. QuickBooks + AI for Accounting

QuickBooks is an AI-powered accounting tool that automates invoicing, tracks expenses, and even generates financial reports. This tool can save hours of manual accounting work.

How You Can Use It:

- Automatically track and categorize business expenses

- Generate financial reports like P&L statements and balance sheets

- Integrate with banks to automatically import transactions

2. Expensify: Automate Expense Management

Expensify uses AI to track and manage expenses. With features like automatic receipt scanning and categorization, it streamlines the process of expense reporting for businesses.

How You Can Use It:

- Automate expense reporting for employees

- Scan and categorize receipts in seconds

- Integrate with QuickBooks or other accounting software for seamless reporting

---

■ Summary: Why AI Is Essential for Business

AI tools can:

- Automate repetitive tasks, saving you time

- Improve decision-making with data-driven insights

- Enhance customer experience with personalized interactions

- Boost marketing efforts with automated content and strategies

◼ Chapter 5: Using ChatGPT & Chatbots

In this chapter, we'll explore how you can use **ChatGPT** and other chatbots to improve communication, enhance customer service, and automate various tasks. Chatbots, powered by AI, are revolutionizing how businesses interact with customers, generate content, and streamline operations.

💬 What Is ChatGPT and Why Should You Use It?

ChatGPT is a language model developed by OpenAI. It's capable of understanding and generating human-like text based on prompts. This makes it an excellent tool for various applications, from content generation to customer support and beyond.

🔍 Key Features of ChatGPT:

- **Natural Language Understanding:** ChatGPT can understand complex queries and generate responses in a conversational manner.

- **Customizable Responses:** You can tailor ChatGPT's output to match the tone, style, and context of your needs.

- **Versatile Use Cases:** From writing blog posts to creating scripts, ChatGPT excels at a variety of content generation tasks.

🚀 How You Can Use ChatGPT in Your Business

1. Content Generation

ChatGPT is a great tool for content creators, marketers, and business owners. It can generate ideas, write articles, create product descriptions, and more.

How You Can Use It:

- **Blog Posts:** Ask ChatGPT to draft blog posts or articles on specific topics.

- **Email Campaigns:** Generate personalized email content to engage your audience.

- **Social Media Posts:** Create engaging and creative posts for platforms like Twitter, Instagram, or LinkedIn.

- **Product Descriptions:** Quickly generate descriptions for new products or services.

Example Prompt: *"Write a 500-word blog post about the benefits of using AI in small businesses."*

2. Customer Support & Engagement

ChatGPT can act as an automated customer support agent, handling common inquiries and providing instant responses. This helps improve efficiency, reduce wait times, and enhance customer experience.

How You Can Use It:

- **FAQ Automation:** Set up ChatGPT to answer frequently asked questions on your website.

- **Instant Support:** Integrate ChatGPT into your live chat systems to provide 24/7 customer support.

- **Lead Qualification:** Use it to qualify leads by asking relevant questions and gathering information about potential customers.

Example Prompt: *"Write an automated response to a customer asking about return policies."*

3. Brainstorming & Idea Generation

Need help coming up with ideas? ChatGPT can help you brainstorm creative ideas for new products, marketing campaigns, blog topics, or even business strategies.

How You Can Use It:

- **Marketing Campaigns:** Get ideas for creative and impactful marketing campaigns.

- **New Products:** Ask ChatGPT to suggest new product ideas based on current market trends.

- **Business Strategies:** Generate strategies for growth, customer retention, and brand awareness.

Example Prompt: *"Give me 10 unique marketing campaign ideas for a new fitness product."*

🛠 How to Use Other Chatbots in Your Business

There are several other AI-powered chatbots that can enhance your business operations. Let's explore a few popular ones:

1. Claude

Claude is a highly advanced chatbot by Anthropic, known for its conversational ability and accuracy. It's designed to generate human-like text responses and can be used for a variety of business purposes.

How You Can Use It:

- Engage in customer conversations

- Answer questions related to products or services

- Generate creative content like newsletters and articles

2. Gemini

Gemini is another AI chatbot that helps businesses with customer interactions, product recommendations, and support.

How You Can Use It:

- Implement it as a personal assistant for your team or customers

- Use it to help customers find products based on their preferences

- Collect customer feedback and insights to improve products/services

3. Perplexity

Perplexity is a chatbot that excels in answering complex queries by using AI to understand context and provide detailed answers.

How You Can Use It:

- Use it to analyze data and give insights

- Automate responses to detailed technical queries

- Help customers with in-depth explanations of products or services

---

▐ Tips for Effective Chatbot Use

1. Be Clear and Specific with Prompts

The quality of your results depends on the clarity of the prompt you provide to the chatbot. The more specific you are, the better the responses will be.

Example: Instead of saying, "Help me write a blog," try "Write a blog post of 500 words about the importance of using AI in business operations."

2. Incorporate Feedback to Improve Chatbot Performance

Chatbots like ChatGPT improve with feedback. If the chatbot's response isn't quite right, refine your prompt or provide additional context.

3. Monitor Interactions and Continuously Improve

It's important to monitor how your chatbots interact with users. Track engagement, identify common questions, and refine your bots' responses based on this data.

⚙ Integrating Chatbots Into Your Website or App

Most chatbot tools, including ChatGPT, offer integration options for websites and apps. This allows you to automate customer support, collect leads, and provide instant assistance to your users.

How You Can Use It:

- **Install Chatbots on Websites:** Add a chatbot to your website to answer visitor questions in real-time.

- **Use in Mobile Apps:** Integrate a chatbot into your mobile app to help users navigate and interact with your app more efficiently.

🎨 Chapter 6: AI in Creative Fields

In this chapter, we'll explore how artificial intelligence is transforming the creative industries, such as writing, design, music production, and video creation. AI-powered tools help artists, content creators, and marketers push their creative boundaries and increase productivity.

📓 AI for Writers and Content Creators

AI tools like **Sudowrite**, **Rytr**, and **Jasper** are changing the game for writers. These tools assist in generating creative content, making writing faster, and helping writers overcome writer's block.

Key Tools for Writers:

- **Sudowrite:** An AI tool designed for creative writers, Sudowrite assists with plot development, brainstorming ideas, and completing stories. It offers helpful prompts, suggestions, and even creative writing prompts.

- **Rytr:** Another powerful tool for content writers, Rytr helps generate copy for blogs, social media posts, advertisements, and more. With multiple writing styles to choose from, Rytr can adjust its tone to fit any audience.

- **Jasper:** Jasper is ideal for marketers and business owners who need help writing SEO-optimized blog posts, emails, and product descriptions. It can write persuasive copy with just a few inputs, speeding up content creation.

How You Can Use These Tools:

- Generate ideas for blog posts, articles, or eBooks

- Write product descriptions and social media content quickly

- Overcome writer's block by receiving AI-generated suggestions

- Create engaging headlines, taglines, and email subject lines

■ AI in Design: Transforming Visual Creativity

AI tools like **Canva AI**, **Midjourney**, and **DALL·E** allow designers to create stunning visuals, graphics, and even logos with minimal effort. AI assists designers by automating repetitive tasks, suggesting design elements, and even creating original artwork.

Key Tools for Designers:

- **Canva AI:** Canva's AI-powered features help users design professional graphics with ease. From auto-generating layouts to resizing images, Canva AI makes graphic design accessible to anyone, regardless of experience.

- **Midjourney:** Midjourney uses AI to generate creative visuals from simple text prompts. Whether you're looking for abstract art or realistic images, Midjourney can bring your ideas to life in minutes.

- **DALL·E:** Created by OpenAI, DALL·E generates images from textual descriptions. Simply describe what you want, and DALL·E will create a visual representation of your idea, making it ideal for marketing, branding, and social media content.

How You Can Use These Tools:

- Create unique social media posts, posters, and website visuals

- Generate logos and branding materials for businesses or personal projects

- Explore AI-generated art for inspiration or to use in creative projects

- Quickly generate product mockups, banners, and marketing materials

---

♪♪ AI in Music Production: Crafting Soundscapes

AI is also making waves in the music industry, enabling musicians and producers to create songs, compositions, and soundscapes with the help of AI tools. Tools like **AIVA** and **Soundraw** allow musicians to generate entire tracks or enhance their creative process.

Key Tools for Music Creators:

- **AIVA (Artificial Intelligence Virtual Artist):** AIVA is an AI composer that helps musicians create original pieces of music. It can generate compositions in a variety of genres, from classical to electronic.

- **Soundraw:** Soundraw is an AI music creation platform that allows users to create and customize music tracks. With a variety of options for tempo, mood, and instruments, Soundraw helps users create high-quality music in minutes.

How You Can Use These Tools:

- Generate background music for videos, presentations, and podcasts

- Create original compositions for personal or commercial use

- Enhance your songwriting by getting AI-generated ideas or full songs

- Customize and remix existing tracks to fit your projects

🎥 AI in Video Production: Making Stunning Visual Content

AI is revolutionizing video production by automating tasks like editing, content generation, and voiceovers. Tools like **Pictory** and **Synthesia** make it easier to create high-quality videos in less time.

Key Tools for Video Creators:

- **Pictory:** Pictory uses AI to automatically edit videos and create YouTube Shorts or long-form videos. It can analyze video content, identify key moments, and even generate subtitles, saving you a lot of time in the editing process.

- **Synthesia:** Synthesia is an AI tool that creates realistic AI-generated avatars that can present your script. It's an excellent tool for creating explainer videos, tutorials, or marketing content without needing a camera crew.

How You Can Use These Tools:

- Quickly create video content for YouTube, social media, and websites

- Generate AI presenters for video scripts or product demos

- Speed up the video editing process by using automatic scene cutting and subtitle generation

- Create educational or promotional videos without requiring professional video production skills

---

🔑 AI in Voiceover and Audio Production

Voice AI tools are now capable of generating lifelike human voices for podcasts, audiobooks, and advertisements. Tools like **Descript** and **WellSaid Labs** are transforming how content creators produce high-quality audio without the need for professional voice actors.

Key Tools for Voiceover Artists:

- **Descript:** Descript allows users to generate and edit podcasts, voiceovers, and audio content using AI. It includes features like transcription, voice cloning, and editing, making it perfect for podcasters or anyone working with spoken word content.

- **WellSaid Labs:** WellSaid Labs specializes in generating high-quality, realistic AI voiceovers. It offers different voice types and accents to create custom audio content for commercial, educational, or entertainment purposes.

How You Can Use These Tools:

- Create AI-generated voiceovers for videos, advertisements, and podcasts

- Transcribe interviews, podcasts, and meetings automatically

- Edit audio content by adjusting tone, pace, and delivery

⚖️ Chapter 7: AI Ethics & Limitations

As AI continues to grow and become more integrated into daily life, it's essential to address the ethical considerations and limitations surrounding its use. While AI offers tremendous opportunities, it also brings up concerns related to bias, privacy, job displacement, and the potential misuse of technology.

🔍 AI Bias

AI systems are only as good as the data they are trained on. If the data contains biases—whether racial, gender-based, or socioeconomic—the AI system can perpetuate those biases, resulting in unfair or discriminatory outcomes.

Examples of AI Bias:

- **Facial Recognition:** AI-based facial recognition systems have shown bias, particularly against people of color. This is often due to the underrepresentation of diverse faces in training datasets.

- **Hiring Algorithms:** Some AI hiring systems have been found to favor male candidates over female candidates or people from certain ethnic backgrounds, based on biased data from past hiring decisions.

How to Address AI Bias:

- Ensure diverse representation in training datasets

- Regularly audit AI systems for bias and fairness

- Use AI systems to complement human decision-making, rather than replace it entirely

🛡 Privacy Concerns with AI

AI can collect, analyze, and store vast amounts of personal data, raising concerns about privacy and security. From social media platforms to smart home devices, AI has access to sensitive information about individuals, and this data can be misused if not properly secured.

\Examples of Privacy Risks:

- **Surveillance:** AI-powered surveillance systems can track and monitor individuals without their knowledge, leading to potential privacy violations.

- **Data Breaches:** AI systems that store personal information may become targets for hackers, resulting in data breaches and identity theft.

How to Protect Privacy:

- Limit the data that AI systems collect and store

- Ensure that AI tools comply with privacy laws like GDPR (General Data Protection Regulation)

- Encrypt sensitive data and implement robust security measures

---

⚙ Job Displacement and Automation

One of the most talked-about concerns regarding AI is its potential to replace human workers. AI's ability to automate tasks traditionally performed by humans has led to fears of widespread job loss in certain sectors, particularly those that involve routine or manual labor.

Industries at Risk:

- **Manufacturing:** Robots and AI systems can handle tasks such as assembly line work, which could replace human labor.

- **Retail:** AI-powered checkout systems and customer service chatbots could replace cashiers and retail workers.

- **Transportation:** Autonomous vehicles could reduce the need for truck drivers, taxi drivers, and delivery personnel.

Mitigating Job Displacement:

- **Upskilling & Reskilling:** Workers should be trained in new skills that complement AI and automation. This could involve learning how to work alongside AI or adopting new roles in fields like data analysis, AI programming, and machine learning.

- **AI as a Complement, Not a Replacement:** Rather than viewing AI as a job destroyer, companies should leverage it as a tool to assist workers, enhancing productivity and allowing employees to focus on more creative or complex tasks.

⚡ AI and Accountability

When AI systems make decisions—especially in critical areas such as healthcare, criminal justice, or finance—it's essential to understand who is responsible for those decisions. If an AI system makes a mistake or causes harm, determining accountability can be tricky.

Examples of Accountability Issues:

- **Autonomous Vehicles:** If a self-driving car causes an accident, who is responsible—the car manufacturer, the software developers, or the owner of the vehicle?

- **Healthcare AI:** If an AI tool incorrectly diagnoses a patient, should the doctor who relied on the AI's advice be held accountable, or is it the fault of the developers?

How to Ensure Accountability:

- Create clear guidelines on who is responsible when AI makes decisions

- Develop AI systems with transparency in mind, so it's clear how and why a decision was made

- Regularly audit AI systems for accuracy, safety, and fairness

● AI's Impact on Society

AI has the potential to transform many aspects of society, from healthcare to education to government. However, its impact will depend largely on how it is implemented, regulated, and monitored.

Positive Impacts:

- **Healthcare:** AI can analyze medical data to assist doctors in diagnosing diseases, discovering new treatments, and personalizing patient care.

- **Education:** AI can provide personalized learning experiences, help teachers automate administrative tasks, and offer tutoring support to students.

- **Environmental Impact:** AI can help address global challenges, such as climate change, by optimizing energy use, improving agricultural practices, and predicting natural disasters.

Negative Impacts:

- **Social Inequality:** If AI benefits only certain sectors of society, it could exacerbate inequality. Those with access to AI technology will have an advantage, while others may be left behind.

- **Dependence on Technology:** Over-reliance on AI could lead to diminished human skills, as people become dependent on AI systems for tasks they once performed themselves.

How to Ensure AI Benefits Society:

- Ensure equitable access to AI tools and benefits

- Regulate AI development to avoid harmful or unethical uses

- Promote collaboration between governments, businesses, and individuals to maximize the positive impact of AI

▲ The Future of AI Ethics

As AI continues to evolve, so too will the ethical considerations surrounding its use. New challenges, such as the development of artificial general intelligence (AGI), could present unforeseen ethical dilemmas.

What Can We Expect?

- **Artificial General Intelligence (AGI):** AGI refers to AI that can perform any intellectual task that a human can. If AGI becomes a reality, it could raise profound ethical questions about autonomy, rights, and control.

- **AI Governance:** We may see more governments and international organizations developing regulations and ethical guidelines to ensure AI is developed and used responsibly.

🛠️ Chapter 8: Beginner AI Projects

Now that you have a basic understanding of AI, it's time to dive into hands-on projects! These beginner-level AI projects will help you get familiar with the tools and concepts, allowing you to experiment with AI in a fun and engaging way.

💬 1. Build a Chatbot Using Chatbase

Creating a simple chatbot is one of the best ways to start working with AI. Chatbots can be used for customer service, answering questions, and even guiding users through processes.

Step-by-Step Guide:

1. **Sign Up on Chatbase:** Go to Chatbase and create an account.

2. **Create Your First Bot:** Choose a template or start from scratch. Chatbase allows you to build conversational flows, add intents, and integrate APIs.

3. **Train Your Bot:** Upload your content and train your chatbot by feeding it different conversation patterns and responses.

4. **Test and Deploy:** Test your chatbot to ensure it works smoothly and deploy it to your website or app.

Project Outcome: By completing this project, you'll learn how to build a basic chatbot that can interact with users, helping businesses automate customer support.

🌐 2. Create AI Art with Midjourney

Midjourney is an AI-powered tool that allows you to create stunning images from text prompts. Whether you want to generate digital art or explore creative designs, Midjourney makes it easy to get started with AI-generated visuals.

Step-by-Step Guide:

1. **Join Midjourney:** Sign up for an account on Midjourney.

2. **Create a Prompt:** Think of something you want to generate. For example, "A futuristic city skyline at sunset."

3. **Input Your Prompt:** Enter your prompt into Midjourney's platform, and the AI will create a unique piece of artwork.

4. **Customize Your Artwork:** Midjourney allows you to tweak and refine your generated images to match your vision.

Project Outcome: By using Midjourney, you'll learn how to use AI to create digital art and gain a deeper understanding of generative models in AI.

📕 3. Create YouTube Shorts with Pictory

Pictory is an AI tool that helps you convert long-form content into short, engaging videos. It's perfect for repurposing your blog posts or videos into shorter, bite-sized clips for platforms like YouTube Shorts, Instagram Reels, and TikTok.

Step-by-Step Guide:

1. **Sign Up on Pictory:** Go to Pictory and sign up for an account.

2. **Upload Your Content:** Upload a blog post or a video that you want to convert into a short video.

3. **Generate Video:** Pictory's AI will automatically extract key points and create a short video based on your content.

4. **Edit and Customize:** Customize the video by adding text, transitions, and background music. You can also adjust the video length and style.

5. **Download and Share:** Once you're happy with the video, download it and upload it to your YouTube Shorts or social media accounts.

Project Outcome: With Pictory, you'll learn how to use AI for video creation and content repurposing, which is an essential skill for content creators and marketers.

📕 4. Build a Recommendation System Using Python

A recommendation system is a type of AI that suggests products, movies, or services based on user preferences. In this project, you'll build a simple recommendation engine using Python.

Step-by-Step Guide:

1. **Install Necessary Libraries:** Use Python libraries like Pandas, NumPy, and Scikit-learn to build the recommendation system.

2. **Prepare Your Dataset:** You can use a dataset from Kaggle or build your own by collecting user data (e.g., product ratings or movie preferences).

3. **Create the Recommendation Engine:** Using collaborative filtering, create a model that suggests items based on user ratings or preferences.

4. **Test and Evaluate:** Test your system with new data and evaluate its accuracy using metrics like Mean Absolute Error (MAE).

Project Outcome: This project will help you understand the basic mechanics of recommendation algorithms and how they can be used in various applications like e-commerce and media streaming services.

🏆 5. Build an Image Classifier Using TensorFlow

TensorFlow is a popular machine learning framework developed by Google, and it's great for building models that can classify images. In this project, you'll create a simple image classifier that can recognize objects in pictures.

Step-by-Step Guide:

1. **Install TensorFlow:** Install the TensorFlow library on your machine by running `pip install tensorflow`.

2. **Get Image Data:** You can use a dataset like CIFAR-10, which contains images of 10 different objects like cars, airplanes, and birds.

3. **Preprocess the Data:** Clean and prepare the images by resizing them and normalizing the pixel values.

4. **Build the Model:** Use a Convolutional Neural Network (CNN) to build a model that can classify the images.

5. **Train and Evaluate:** Train the model using the dataset and evaluate its accuracy.

Project Outcome: By completing this project, you'll gain hands-on experience with deep learning techniques, specifically convolutional neural networks, and learn how to apply them to image classification tasks.

🎙 6. Voice Assistant with Google Speech API

Voice assistants like Siri, Alexa, and Google Assistant are powered by AI that understands voice commands. In this project, you'll use Google's Speech-to-Text API to build a basic voice assistant that can understand and respond to simple commands.

Step-by-Step Guide:

1. **Set Up Google Cloud:** Sign up for a Google Cloud account and enable the Speech-to-Text API.

2. **Install Required Libraries:** Use Python and install libraries like `speech_recognition` and `gTTS` (Google Text-to-Speech) for speech recognition and synthesis.

3. **Create the Assistant:** Write a Python script that listens for voice commands, converts them into text, and performs actions (e.g., telling the time, opening a website).

4. **Customize Your Assistant:** Add more features like weather updates, news, or controlling smart devices.

Project Outcome: You'll learn how to work with speech recognition and text-to-speech technologies to build your own voice assistant, which is a valuable skill for AI developers.